MW01065502

DANIEL *Boone*

Our People

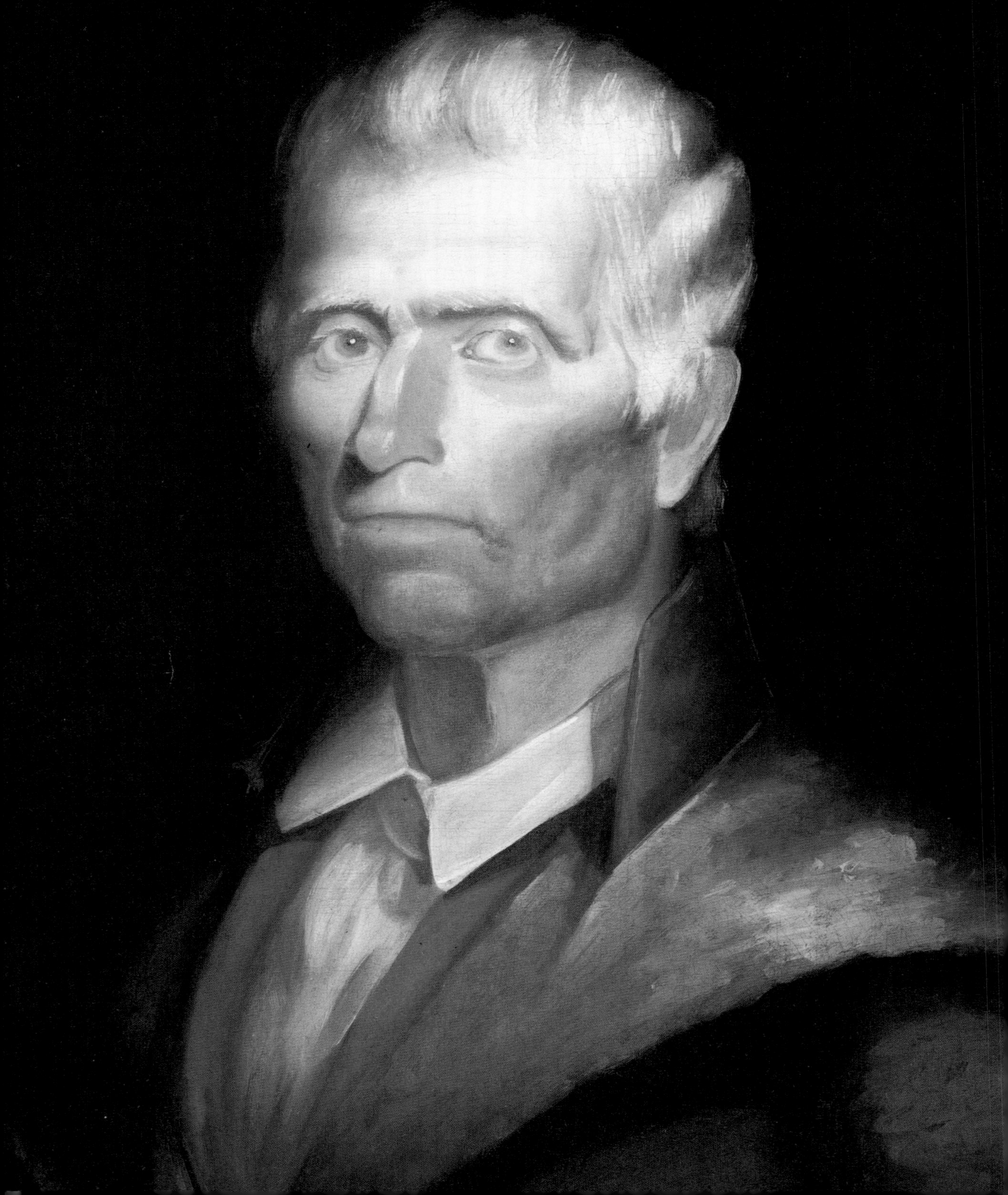

SPIRIT
of America®

DANIEL *Boone*

FRONTIERSMAN

By Judy Alter

The Child's World®
Chanhassen, Minnesota

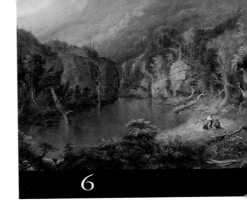

6

Daniel Boone

Published in the United States of America by The Child's World®
PO Box 326 • Chanhassen, MN 55317-0326 • 800-599-READ • www.childsworld.com

Acknowledgments
The Child's World®: Mary Berendes, Publishing Director

Editorial Directions, Inc.: E. Russell Primm, Emily Dolbear, and Lucia Raatma, Editors; Linda S. Koutris, Photo Selector; Dawn Friedman, Photo Research; Red Line Editorial, Fact Research; Irene Keller, Copy Editor; Tim Griffin/IndexServ, Indexer; Chad Rubel, Proofreader

Photos
Cover: National Portrait Gallery, Smithsonian Institution/Art Resource; National Portrait Gallery, Smithsonian Institution/Art Resource: 2; Bettmann/Corbis: 7, 12, 21; Corbis: 9, 24; David Muench/Corbis: 13; Gianni Dagli Orti/Corbis: 15; Raymond Gehman/Corbis: 28; Hulton Archive/Getty Images: 8, 11 bottom, 16, 19; Library of Congress: 10; North Wind Picture Archives: 14, 17 top, 17 bottom, 18, 22, 25, 26; Stock Montage: 23, 27.

Registration
The Child's World®, Spirit of America®, and their associated logos are the sole property and registered trademarks of The Child's World®.

Library of Congress Cataloging-in-Publication Data
Alter, Judy, 1938–
  Daniel Boone : frontiersman / by Judy Alter.
      p. cm.
  Includes bibliographical references and index.
  Summary: Provides a brief introduction to Daniel Boone, his accomplishments, and his impact on American history.
   ISBN 1-56766-162-9 (lib. bdg. : alk. paper)
  1. Boone, Daniel, 1734–1820—Juvenile literature. 2. Pioneers—Kentucky—Biography—Juvenile literature. 3. Frontier and pioneer life—Kentucky—Juvenile literature. 4. Kentucky—Biography—Juvenile literature. 5. Kentucky—Discovery and exploration—Juvenile literature. [1. Boone, Daniel, 1734–1820. 2. Pioneers.] I. Title.
  F454.B66 A79 2002
  976.9'02'092—dc21

                                2001007396

12   14   23

92
B644a

2/04

Contents

Child's World   18.95

Chapter ONE

Opening the American West

IN THE 1770S, THE LAND THAT LAY WEST OF the Appalachian Mountains was the American West. The Appalachian Mountains run from Canada in the north to Alabama in the south. Early American settlers lived between the Atlantic Ocean and those mountains. Beyond the mountains, Native Americans controlled the land.

Daniel Boone is known for finding a pass through the Cumberland Mountains.

People call Daniel Boone a hero because he brought settlers across the Appalachian Mountains. He opened the land that is now Kentucky to settlers. Boone is considered the first great **frontiersman** of the United States.

Boone was known as a "long hunter." He was called that because he carried a long, or Kentucky, rifle. During his lifetime, he was a hunter, a trapper, and an officer in the **militia**. He was once captured by Shawnee Indians. With no real education, he was elected three times to the Virginia government.

In this engraving, a rifleman aims his long rifle.

Daniel Boone had many jobs during his life. He worked as a **surveyor**. He also made money by selling land and running a **tavern**. He went from having a great fortune to being deeply in debt. Daniel Boone spent his last years doing what he loved best—hunting. He died a poor man in Missouri.

Opening the frontier cost Boone dearly. His son, James, was attacked and killed by the Shawnee in 1773. The same Indians kidnapped

Interesting Fact

▶ Kentucky was once called the "Dark and Bloody Ground" because of the fierce fighting between settlers and Native Americans during the late 1770s.

his daughter, Jemima, and two friends in 1776. The girls were rescued after several terrifying days. His son, Israel, was killed in 1782 at the Battle of Blue Licks. That was one of the last major battles of the Revolutionary War.

Daniel Boone loved the wilderness.

Daniel Boone was a true woods-man. He could always find peace in the wilderness. Often he went there for years at a time, leaving behind his wife, Rebecca, and his ten children. Life in the forest may have been more impor-tant to him than everything he did to earn his fame.

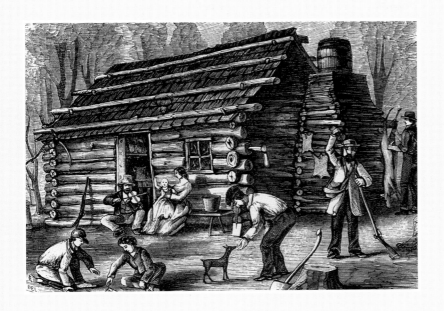

STORIES SAY REBECCA Boone was very beautiful. She is said to have been angry at Boone's long trips far from home. Some say she lived in fear that he might be killed in the wilderness.

Actually, Rebecca Boone was an independent woman who got along very well by herself. Like many pioneer women, she worked hard in the house and on the land (above). When Daniel was away, she took care of her garden and chopped wood. She gave birth to her 10 children and brought them up. She once shot seven deer from a tree in one day to feed her family!

In 1765, Daniel Boone explored Florida. One story says he traded skins for a house in Pensacola, Florida. When he returned home, he told his wife that the family was moving to Florida. Rebecca refused to go, and Daniel never discussed it again.

When Boone opened a tavern in Kentucky, Rebecca ran it. She was proud of his work in the Virginia government. When Boone ran out of luck and money, Rebecca lived with him in the wilderness without complaint. Rebecca Boone died in Missouri in 1813.

Chapter TWO

A Love of the Wilderness

DANIEL BOONE WAS BORN ON NOVEMBER 2, 1734, in Berks County, Pennsylvania. He was one of 11 children. His parents were Sarah and Squire Boone. His father came from England. He worked as a weaver and a **blacksmith** and also raised cattle.

As a boy, Daniel went into the wilderness to look after his father's cattle. He learned to live in the woods. He studied the animals and the peaceful Indians in the area. At the age of 12, he was given a rifle and he learned to hunt. He began to sell the hides of the deer he shot. He also learned to be a blacksmith, so that he could help his father.

In 1734, Daniel Boone was born in this house in Pennsylvania.

The Boone family were Quakers. In 1750, the Quakers **disowned** Squire Boone for allowing one of his daughters to marry out of the faith. The family left Pennsylvania. They settled in a valley on the Yadkin River in western North Carolina.

In 1755, when he was 20, Boone marched with American volunteers and British soldiers. They attacked the French at Fort Duquesne on the Ohio River. The French, fighting alongside the Native Americans, beat the British soldiers.

In 1755, Native Americans attacked British troops at Fort Duquesne.

Making his way home alone, Daniel was attacked by a drunken Indian. Boone killed the man while defending himself. The event upset him so much that he didn't tell anyone about it.

Daniel married Rebecca Bryan in 1756. They settled in the Yadkin Valley. When Native Americans began raiding the valley, they moved to Virginia. Daniel built a cabin, planted corn, and took off west to hunt. This became the pattern of his life. He planted in the spring and summer, hunted in the autumn, and trapped beaver in the winter.

Boone made many trips west. His first major trip was in 1769. He took an explorer named John Finley west. Boone knew how to explore by then. He took riding and pack animals, kettles, blankets, salt, and rum. He also took lead, gunpowder, and extra guns.

In the wilderness, men built cabins out of logs.

Daniel's brother, Squire, joined the party. They crossed the Cumberland Gap. The Cumberland Gap is a natural pass through the Appalachian Mountains, near the spot where Virginia, Kentucky, and Tennessee meet. They made camp near a branch of the Kentucky River.

The Cumberland Gap as it looks today

In a short time, they had collected a wealth of hides to trade back east. Shawnee Indians stole their hides and their horses. Boone and his group were able to recover the horses, but then the Shawnee captured them. After two days, the Native Americans let them go free and ordered them never to return. Finley returned to the east. The Boone brothers stayed in Kentucky to hunt.

In May 1770, Squire Boone went east with enough hides to pay their debts. Daniel rode alone to explore western Kentucky. He had no salt, no sugar, and no flour. He slept without a fire to avoid capture by Native Americans. When Squire returned later, the

13

Daniel Boone is wearing his familiar cap and holding his long rifle.

two men hunted again and then headed home. Once again, the Native Americans stole their horses, furs, and rifles.

Daniel Boone returned home in 1771. By then, he believed he could make a fortune in the **bluegrass** country of Kentucky. It was a hunter's paradise.

In 1773, he decided to move his family across the mountains to Kentucky. Five other families went with them. They took cattle and supplies to start a community. Boone's son, 16-year-old son, James, and some friends trailed behind the main group.

Near the Cumberland Gap, Native Americans attacked the boys and killed James. One of the boys told Daniel Boone about the attack. Boone rode back to bury his son. The group returned to Virginia.

14

QUAKERS ARE ALSO KNOWN AS THE RELIGIOUS SOCIETY OF FRIENDS. The society began in England in the 1600s. A man named George Fox believed that everyone, not just bishops and priests, had a personal relationship with God. Quakers believe all people have an inner voice that reflects their relationship with God. At Quaker meetings, members sit silently until one or another is moved to speak.

Quakers have always opposed war. They believe that faith in Christ has been given to all people everywhere. They also believe that men and women have equal status in worship.

Today, a Quaker would not be disowned if a child married out of the faith. In the 1700s, however, the practice was not uncommon.

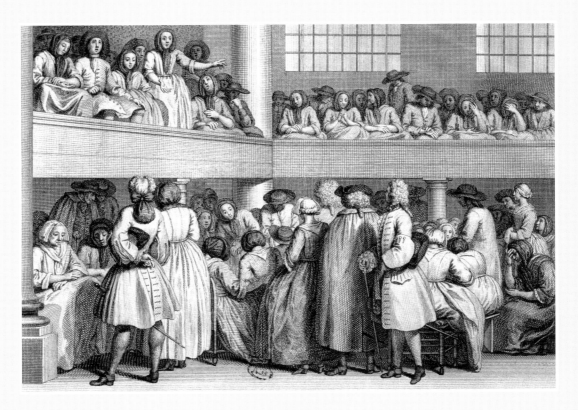

Chapter THREE

Defending Boonesborough

In this famous painting by George Caleb Bingham, Daniel Boone leads settlers through the Cumberland Gap.

IN MARCH 1775, DANIEL BOONE SET OFF with 30 men to build a road across the Cumberland Gap. They made a fort of small shacks on the Kentucky River.

Richard Callaway, a neighbor of Boone's in Virginia, became the group's unofficial leader. He set up the government of Transylvania. The settlements of Boonesborough, Harrodsburg, and Logan Station were also set up. Because of problems with the Virginia government and the Revolutionary

War, the government of Transylvania did not last. But its settlements survived. Boone brought his family to Boonesborough.

By then, the French had left the region. The colonies considered England the enemy. The British encouraged the Shawnee warriors to attack the settlements. They gave the Indians supplies, arms, and liquor in exchange for fighting the settlers.

Covered wagons crossing a river

In 1776, on a Sunday afternoon, Jemima Boone and Richard Callaway's daughters, Fanny and Betsey, went for a canoe ride. Shawnees kidnapped them on the Kentucky River near Boonesborough. Daniel Boone led the party that rescued the terrified girls several days later.

Daniel Boone rescued his daughter and her two friends from Indians in 1776.

By 1778, some settlers had returned to Virginia. Others

A drawing of Fort Boonesborough

Interesting Fact

▶ Most stories say that Daniel Boone killed dozens of Indians. Boone claimed to have killed only three Indians in his entire life—in defense of himself.

went back to Boonesborough. The overcrowded settlement ran low on basic supplies, including salt. Daniel Boone led a trip to salt springs called Blue Licks. They boiled the salty river water to extract the salt. It would take many weeks to make enough salt for the settlement.

One day while Boone and a few others were hunting deer, the Shawnee captured them. Boone was a prize for the Indians because he was well known. But they also admired his fighting and woodsman skills.

A chief named Blackfish adopted Boone. In a special ceremony, Boone was dressed and painted like an Indian. He spent four months with Blackfish before escaping and returning to Boonesborough.

In 1778, the Battle of Boonesborough took place between Blackfish and his men and the settlers. The Native Americans outnumbered the men in the fort. The Shawnee tried to starve the people out of the fort. Then they tried to burn them out. Because rain had dampened the wood of the **stockade**, it would not burn.

Boonesborough settlers defend themselves against the Shawnee.

The Shawnee even tried to dig a tunnel from the river to the stockade. The settlers dug a tunnel to meet the Shawnee's tunnel at right angles. They planned to kill the Native Americans one at a time as they came through.

On the ninth night, a heavy rainstorm hit the area. The Shawnee tunnel collapsed, and the Native Americans left in disgust. The next morning, the Native Americans were gone.

Then Richard Callaway turned against Boone. He charged Boone with siding with the Shawnee and teaming up with the British. By saving Fort Boonesborough, Boone had in fact strengthened the position of the new United States in the West. As long as the settlements remained, it would be hard for the British to push Americans back across the Appalachians. Boone was finally cleared of all charges. He was promoted from captain to major in the militia.

But Daniel Boone was very angry with Callaway. He had rescued Callaway's daughters from kidnappers. His daughter, Jemima, was married to one of Callaway's sons. He left Boonesborough in disgust.

IN DANIEL BOONE'S DAY, KENTUCKY WAS GOVERNED BY AUGUSTA County, Virginia. In 1772, Fincastle County, Virginia, was organized. It included all of what is now the state of Kentucky.

In 1792, Kentucky joined the Union as a state. It was the first state from the western frontier to join. Only four U.S. states, including Kentucky, are called commonwealths. The word *commonwealth* means "government based on the common approval of the people."

Kentucky is the birthplace of 16th U.S. president Abraham Lincoln. During the Civil War, the problem of slavery divided the state. Wealthy landowners supported slavery. Small farmers and mountain families did not. Although most people in Kentucky supported the Union, the Confederacy tried to claim the territory.

After the Civil War, Kentucky produced coal, tobacco, and racehorses. Today, the state is known for its thoroughbred racing horses. The state horse is the thoroughbred. Kentucky is also known for Fort Knox, where U.S. gold is stored (above).

Kentucky is nicknamed the Bluegrass State. The state song is "My Old Kentucky Home."

Chapter FOUR

Fame and Ruin

An older Daniel Boone
with his rifle and dog

DANIEL BOONE FOUNDED BOONE'S STATION. With $20,000 of his own money and $30,000 from friends, he rode to Richmond to buy bluegrass land. While he slept in an inn on the way, a thief stole the money from his saddlebags. Boone was very upset, but his friends supported him as a man of honor.

Bad luck continued. His son, Israel, was a member of the militia. Near Blue Licks, Israel's unit planned to charge the Shawnees. Boone knew the tricks of the enemy, and he expected a surprise attack.

He warned the militia to wait for support.
One lieutenant colonel laughed at Boone
and boasted that his men were not cowards.
Israel was killed in the five-minute battle
that followed. Boone never recovered from
the guilt of not having prevented the attack.

Daniel Boone fights over the body of his son at Blue Licks in 1782.

This early map of Kentucky Territory was created in 1784.

In 1782, a Pennsylvania schoolteacher named John Filson bought a great deal of land in Kentucky. Then he wrote a book called *The Discovery, Settlement and present state of Kentucke*. It sold in enormous numbers throughout the colonies.

One part of the book was called *The Adventures of Col. Daniel Boon.* Filson wrote it as a personal account from Daniel Boone. But Daniel Boone would never have written in such an overly educated and affected manner. There were errors in the stories, too. Unpleasant events, such as the death of James, were left out. Filson wanted to encourage people to buy land in Kentucky, not scare them away.

Daniel Boone became famous as a hero of the wilderness. He was also in demand as an explorer and surveyor. Easterners wanted him to locate and survey land for them to buy in the Kentucky bluegrass country. Boone insisted that half of any land he surveyed be deeded to him.

Today, visitors can follow the Daniel Boone Trail through the Appalachian Mountains.

Interesting Fact

▶ *The Adventures of Col. Daniel Boon* by John Filson was published as a separate book in the U.S. and several foreign countries.

*Portrait of
Daniel Boone*

Soon, Boone claimed 50,000 acres (20,250 hectares) in his own name. He was now a man of wealth and property. He was elected to the Virginia government. He opened a tavern at Limestone on the Ohio River. He also dealt in skins, furs, horses, and occasionally, slaves. But Boone had made a mistake. He still thought of the land as open and free. He did not think in terms of courts and lawyers. After he surveyed land, he didn't bother to register the deeds. Boone, like many others, lost his land to settlers who had set up homesteads and registered deeds on it. Boone, once a hero, was now thought of as a cheater. He tried to sell land to pay his debts but found he had little land to sell.

By the mid 1790s, he and Rebecca were living in the woods again, with two of their daughters and their husbands. They had

Daniel Boone lived with his family in Kentucky for some years.

This stone detail from his grave monument shows Daniel Boone fighting a Native American.

almost nothing left. Boone eventually left Kentucky because he could not pay his debts.

Daniel Boone moved to Missouri in 1799, following his son, Daniel. For the next 20 years, he hunted. Once he traveled as far west as the Yellowstone River. Daniel Boone died in 1820 at the age of 86. He is buried near Frankfort, Kentucky.

1734 Daniel Boone is born on November 2 in Berks County, Pennsylvania.

1750 The Boone family moves to North Carolina.

1755 Boone fights with American volunteers and British regulars against the French at Fort Duquesne. He kills a Native American in self-defense.

1756 Boone marries Rebecca Bryan.

1769 Boone's first major expedition travels west over the Appalachian Mountains.

1771 Boone returns home from his first trip.

1773 Boone decides to move his family to Kentucky territory. Boone's son, James, is killed near Cumberland Gap. Boone takes his family back to North Carolina.

1775 Boone takes 30 men to build a road across the Cumberland Gap. Boone's family settles in Boonesborough.

1776 Jemima Boone and two friends are kidnapped by Shawnee Indians.

1778 Boone is captured by the Shawnee while he is hunting near Blue Licks salt springs. The Battle of Boonesborough is fought. Boone is robbed of $50,000 with which he was going to file claim on land in Kentucky.

1782 Boone's son, Israel, is killed in an ambush near Blue Licks. John Filson publishes *The Discovery, Settlement and present state of Kentucke*, which makes Daniel Boone a national hero.

1790s Boone, heavily in debt, moves to the woods with his wife Rebecca, their two daughters, and their daughters' husbands.

1799 Daniel and Rebecca Boone move to Missouri.

1820 Daniel Boone dies at the age of 86.

Glossary TERMS

blacksmith (BLAK-smith)
A blacksmith makes and fits horse-shoes and repairs iron tools. Daniel Boone's father was a blacksmith.

bluegrass (BLOO-grass)
Bluegrass is a grass with a slightly blue tint. In large pastures in spring, it appears to be a rich blue color. Bluegrass country is a region in central Kentucky known for its horse farms and its beautiful fields of bluegrass.

disowned (diss-OHND)
Someone who is disowned is cast out of a family or group. The Quakers disowned Daniel Boone's father.

frontiersman (fruhn-TEERZ-man)
A frontiersman explores the far edge of a settled land, where few people live. Daniel Boone is considered to be one of the greatest frontiersmen in American history.

militia (muh-LISH-uh)
A militia is a group of citizens trained to fight in emergencies. Boone was once an officer in a militia.

stockade (stawk-AYD)
A stockade is a strong fence used to protect against attacks. The Shawnee tried to burn the stockade of the fort during the Battle of Boonesborough.

surveyor (sur-VAY-uhr)
A surveyor charts land to draw a map or make a plan. Daniel Boone once worked as a surveyor.

tavern (TAV-ern)
A tavern is a public place where people go to buy alcoholic drinks. Rebecca Boone ran her husband's tavern in Kentucky.

For Further INFORMATION

Web Sites

Visit our homepage for lots of links about Daniel Boone:
http://www.childsworld.com/links.html

Note to Parents, Teachers, and Librarians:
We routinely verify our Web links to make sure they're safe,
active sites—so encourage your readers to check them out!

Books

Calvert, Patricia. *Daniel Boone: Beyond the Mountains.* Tarrytown, N.Y.:
Benchmark Books, 2001.

Chambers, Catherine E. *Daniel Boone and the Wilderness Road.* Mahwah, N.J.:
Troll, 1998.

Green, Carl R., and William R. Sanford. *Daniel Boone: Wilderness Pioneer.*
Springfield, N.J.: Enslow Publishers, Inc., 1997.

Kozar, Richard. *Daniel Boone and the Exploration of the Frontier.* Bromall,
Penn.: Chelsea House, 2000.

Places to Visit or Contact

Daniel Boone Homestead
To learn about Daniel Boone's early life
400 Daniel Boone Road
Birdsboro, PA 19508
610-582-4900

Fort Boonesborough State Park
To visit Daniel Boone's working fort complete with blockhouses, cabins,
and period furnishings
4375 Boonesborough Road
Richmond, KY 40475-9316
859-527-3131

Index